The Gift *of* Clarity

*40 Practical Recipes to Discover
Your Will, Define Your Goals,
and Make a Change*

ROMEM SARANGA

Production by eBookPro Publishing
www.ebook-pro.com

The Gift of Clarity
Romem Saranga

Copyright © 2024 Romem Saranga

All rights reserved; no parts of this book may be reproduced or transmitted in any form or by any means, electronic or mechanical, including photocopying, recording, taping, or by any information retrieval system, without the permission, in writing, of the author.

Translation: Rosanne Fix
Contact: romem.s@gmail.com

ISBN 9798300743529

"Sell your cleverness and buy bewilderment."

Rumi

CONTENTS

Introduction

Recommended reading 13

Part I: From Moment to Moment

Clarity in Daily Desires in Real Time: "What Do I Want Now?" 21

    1. Doing the dishes 22

    2. Mindless Wandering 24

    3. A Glass of Decaffeinated Water 26

    4. Media Cleanse 27

    5. Tasks in the Oven 29

    6. Ten Extra Minutes 31

    7. Stop and Look Back 32

    8. Worry Neutralizing Chai Masala 34

    9. Sitting 36

    10. Get Out of Bed and Out of the House 38

    11. Fog Lights 39

    12. Today I'm a Prince 41

Part II: New Revelations

Recipes that Reveal New Desires 43

    13. First Time 44

    14. The Other Alternative 46

    15. Going Out with a Friend 48

    16. Coincidental conversations 50

    17. Unfamiliar music 52

    18. A Couple of Hours by the Sea 54

    19. Total Boredom 56

    20. What Don't I Want? 58

    21. While You Were Angry 60

    22. Aspire like the One You Admire 62

    23. Poor Man, Rich Man 64

    24. Observing a Holy Day. Or Thursday 67

Part III: Exploring the Depths of our Consciousness

Reinforcing the Foundations of Our Will and Strengthening Desire 69

    25. Playing Backgammon 70

    26. Turning "Need" Into "Want" 72

    27. Keeping a journal 74

    28. Taking a Hike 76

    29. A Month in a Foreign City 78

    30. Four Days in the Country 84

    31. Playing Like a Child 86

32. Consciously Listen to Music 88

33. Artistic Endeavors 90

34. The Spiritual Path 92

35. Maybe You Should Talk to Someone 94

36. Contractions of the Will 97

37. Desire Under Investigation 101

38. Kicking the Cheese 103

39. Equalizing Identities 106

40. Ask "What do I Want?" 109

Hints

Five Hints for the Question "What Do I Want?" 111

Hint No. 1: I Want to Live 112

Hint No. 2: I want to Be Free 114

Hint No. 3: I want to Be Happy 116

Hint No. 4: I want to Do Good 119

Hint No. 5: I Want Free Will 121

Epilogue: 7 minutes in Heaven 123

Acknowledgements 125

PROLOGUE

One Friday in January, in line for coffee, I met Yoav. Yoav is the founder and owner of "The Thai Underground", a renowned Thai restaurant in my town. A few years ago, "The Thai Underground" really was an underground, a small street stall open for just a few hours a day, a couple of times a week. Word got around and not much later the underground became an empire, a big successful place open daily, known to all. I met Yoav during the transition from small to large. Our acquaintance was superficial, yet even then I could sense that Yoav, though happy with his success, was looking for something new and different, looking for the next thing. Several years later, in that line for coffee, I skipped the perfunctory hellos and boldly asked: "So, what's the next thing?"

Yoav was unfazed by my direct question. He said he didn't know. That he was still looking. He then asked me about my book. Unsure of which book he was referring to, I spoke proudly of the books I had published. The first was a cookbook for men who don't cook called "Dad Can Cook Too", which had by then received its share of success. Yoav was unimpressed. He said the problem wasn't how to cook, the problem was deciding what to cook. **"We don't know**

what we want," he said. "True." I said, and added, half in jest, that perhaps that would be the topic of my next book....

It was only after a few hours of cooking (I had managed to decide to make stuffed peppers) that I laid down on the couch and closed my eyes. I recalled my conversation with Yoav, his thoughts and comments and my idea for a new book. Suddenly I could see the new book materializing before my eyes. It would be a recipe book! Just like "Dad Can Cook Too" except that now it would be "Dad Knows What He Wants Too!" Every recipe would be a path, a method, a tactic that would help me uncover and find my will, that which I want most. I started to think of "recipes" I had discovered over the years and realized I had something to offer, a collection I can share.

I wish someone had given me a book like this a few years ago. **I have always struggled with the question "What do I want?"** For many years it hardly bothered me. Even without a clear sense of what I wanted, life led me to good places. Sometimes it led me to a crisis, where things I didn't want became apparent, but I nearly never had a clear, strong desire. (Lucky for me, the woman by my side knew exactly what she wanted, because even to the question of having children I never said "Yes!" My answer was more like "Well, Okay, one kid, then we'll see...")

In the last few years, I started to feel that my inability to answer the question "What do I want?" is taking a toll on my personal happiness. Truth be told, I've never really been a joyful man. I tended to take life seriously, and I didn't laugh or smile much. Sometimes my expression was so severe that my youngest daughter, then three years old, started to say "Smile Daddy." That's how bad it was. I remember one moment in particular. I was out walking the dog, head down, steps heavy. My dog stopped outside Feldenstein's grocery store to pee on a bush and I thought to myself: "Well, Romem, you're not a happy person. You should just accept it."

But I guess I didn't accept it, because something began to change, and **the first question which triggered this change was the question "What do I want?"**. For the first time in my life I felt that it might be right to find an answer. To start searching. But how? How can I know what I want? I didn't know where to start. After years of neglect, the path to my will was obscured.

Well, not completely obscured. There's always a crack. Once I started to ask myself "What do I want?" I became aware of inklings of will, and I noticed tricks and tools that could help me enlarge the crack and reveal more of my desire. The more I asked and the more I honed and perfected my skills, I discovered more and more desires: small quotidian desires, new and surprising desires, even deep and meaningful desires that could change the course of my life. **I learned that having clarity about what I want is a great source of joy.** When I know what I want and can connect to the source of my will, I'm a free and happy man. Today, when I walk down the street with my dog, my back is straight and my steps are light. When he stops to pee on the bush outside of Feldenstein's I say to myself, "It's only been a few years since you stood here thinking that you're not a happy person…. Look at yourself now!"

How to use this book?

I am positive that every one of you, my will-challenged fellows, is able to find their own flowing source of desire, and that the recipes in this book can help. You'll find recipes that will provoke deep thought, and recipes that will tell you to do the dishes; recipes that will send you out into the world, and recipes that will direct you to explore your inner self; recipes that will alter your consciousness, and recipes for the time you are waiting in line…. All these recipes have served, and still serve me well, and I continue to use them daily.

This is a recipe book, and like in any cookbook, you are free to pick and choose recipes. There is no particular order to follow and not every recipe will appeal to every person. I invite you to choose recipes that you find interesting and that you would like to try. Feel free to make alterations so that the recipes are more to your liking. Basically — do what you want! And if you don't know what you want… Well, you have 40 recipes to help you figure that out!

INTRODUCTION

Recommended reading

1. Inquiring of God — Foundations of Talmudic & Biblical Psychology, Dr. Yair Caspi

I was already deep in the process of writing the recipes for this book when I felt the need for a few days on my own. I needed both the time to work on my book and the quiet to hear myself better. I did "Four days in the country" (recipe no.30) and went to the desert. The small hotel I stayed in had a bookshelf with an eclectic collection of books. They were arranged by color. I scanned the books with my eyes, but my hand never left my pocket to reach out for any of the books. I was about to turn away when something made me turn back to the white books, and the title "Inquiring of God" caught my eye. **Before I knew why — my hand reached out and took the book off its shelf.** I went through it quickly, looking, as usual, not only at the first few pages, but at the end too, when there, in chapter 39, I saw the title: *What do I want?*

And the rest is history.

You don't have to read all the way to chapter 39 in order to understand the relevance of this book. It is relevant from the introduction onward. Dr. Caspi's exploration of Judaic Psychology is fascinating. In his book, which is divided into sections called Portals, Caspi investigates, among other topics, the issue of will, and the unearthing of our desires. In chapter 13 Caspi makes this clear observation:

"What do I want? For some this is an easy question. Their desires are right at the surface of consciousness. They may have grown up in families that allowed them to desire, to hear their own voice, to make demands. They were allowed to acknowledge their instincts and experience their sexuality.

Some people don't know what they want. Will, they were taught, leads us astray; yielding to passion results in self-destruction. When asked what they want, they answer in terms of what they are allowed to want; what is acceptable; the right thing to do. They are deaf to their will but hear the call of duty. They were probably raised in families where needs and sexual instincts and the development of their own unique voice were strictly forbidden. They lived in families that knew only how to make demands."

In chapter 15 He goes on to say:

"Withdrawal: Hearing our internal voice and letting it sound forth so it will be heard by the One who is always attuned to it. In order to identify my own voice I have to differentiate it from the voices of society and family. In order to do so, I may need to go away, someplace peaceful where I won't be both-

ered by the noises in the street, or distracted by television, books, newspapers, telephones and computers: a Temple."

And in chapter 39 he suggests asking oneself three questions that will lead the reader on *"The Path of Desire"*:

A. *What do I want?*

B. *What is my evil inclination?* [our evil inclinations can serve as a gateway to our will]

C. *What element of truth is inherent to my desires?* [appropriate intentions can be expressed through your evil inclinations too]

Dr. Yair Caspi offers the reader a deep, brave and thorough exploration of the psyche, and some strong statements. He invites us to do inner work, but offers no recipes. In a way, this recipe book complements Dr. Caspi's book, like a workbook complementing a textbook. And vice-versa, Caspi's analysis and deep probing questions serve as a psychological and philosophical basis for the question of the discovery of our will which this recipe book addresses in a practical manner.

2. Awakening joy: 10 Steps That Will Put You on the Road to Real Happiness, James Baraz and Shoshana Alexander

Those of you who find the word "God" a turn off, are deterred by the call for inner work, and disapprove of strong statements, will certainly find joy in James Baraz's book.

James is one of the best and gentlest teachers I know. He teaches mindfulness and has a unique wisdom about all things related to joy. He is both a joyful man, and a wise man, and has been teaching courses on personal happiness since 2003. When I told him about my idea for this book, he was very enthusiastic and sent me to read the first and last chapters of his book. I'm sending you to read all the chapters in the middle too, but do start with the introduction, because the introduction is both wonderful and inviting.

Like Yair Caspi, James Baraz also suggests inner work, But **the gentle way he suggests doing it will dissolve any objection.** You will not find any mention of God in this book (only as an alternative word like Dharma, the Cosmos, or Life), and the tools he offers are readily available, simple, and inviting. This is not a book about discovering your will, but it is a book about discovering happiness, and some of the paths to happiness go through discovering one's will and desires.

3. The Art of Loving, Erich Fromm

In this book, Erich Fromm writes nearly 100 pages of an Intellectual-Philosophical "Introduction" on love, art, and contemporary western society, followed by twenty pages of practical advice. Almost 100 pages of gripping, bitter, discouraging and slightly humorous analysis (at least that's how I chose to read it, with a smile…), which lead to the main topic: A practical guide to the mastery of the art of loving.

This "introduction" opens an intellectual gate within which we can perceive not only society, but mainly ourselves. I invite you to read the book and stop to occasionally ask yourself where you stand, personally, in lieu of his statements; Where do you see yourself in his analysis of human prototypes and personal inclinations; How do you perceive yourself in his view of how people practice or avoid love.

How is love related to will? **Fromm does not speak of will directly, but I sense that love is, at least, indirectly connected to our will, and probably directly connected with it.**

He writes on page 101:

"The most important step in learning concentration [...a necessary condition for the mastery of an art, including the art of loving...] is to learn to be alone with oneself [without reading, listening to the radio, smoking or drinking]. Indeed, to be able to concentrate means to be able to be alone with oneself—and this ability is precisely a condition for the ability to love. If I am attached to another person because I cannot stand on my own feet, he or she may be a lifesaver, but the relationship is not one of love. Paradoxically, the ability to be alone is the condition for the ability to love."

When you understand love better and especially when you practice the art of loving as Fromm invites us to, you reinforce your ability to be alone. The ability to be alone, in its turn, develops your ability for self-listening, self-sensitivity and self-knowledge which will lead to an understanding of what, for heaven's sake, that self really wants.

Indeed, everything is connected to everything: In order to master the art of love, Fromm recommends mindfulness; Baraz recommends the discovery of one's desires in order to awaken joy; And God ties in with both Love and Goodwill, as the blessing for the Sabbath says: "and [He] has given us, in love and goodwill, His holy Sabbath…"

Presented with Love and Goodwill

PART I:
FROM MOMENT TO MOMENT

Clarity in Daily Desires in Real Time: "What Do I Want *Now*?"

Our desires tend to be obscured by daily tasks and commitments, driven below our level of consciousness. Barely seen and heard, they are easy to forget. The rationale behind these recipes is simple: Easily done recipes made to clear up some quiet time and space for our free will to manifest.

1. Doing the dishes

Dishwashing is like brainwashing in a good way. This recipe is best for times when you're feeling confused, scattered and disconnected, and have no idea what to do with yourself.

Ingredients:

A sink full of dishes

Soap, sponge and a dish rack

Hot water

Directions:

1 Prepare the area: clear the room of people so that you don't need to speak to anybody and turn off all media so that you don't have to listen to anything.

2 Wash the dishes with soap, a sponge and hot water.

   Do not use the dishwasher! Handwash the dishes slowly and thoughtfully.

3 Don't try to be efficient. Wash the dishes calmly, taking at least 45 minutes. **Your objective is not cleaning the dishes as much as cleansing your mind,** removing harmful, useless thoughts and enabling clarity (just as you are cleaning the glass you're washing, rendering it crystal clear).

4   There is no need for mental activity or effort. You don't need to exert force to cleanse your mind. You take care of the dishes, and your mind will clean itself. Yes, your mind has a self-cleaning program, and doing the dishes is the way to activate it.

5   If you're disturbed by obsessive thoughts — never mind! They may not really be "'disturbing", they might be a part of the cleansing process. Here are two suggestions to help you ease your mind: Try to concentrate on what you're doing ("Here I am soaping a plate...now I'm washing this glass...wow! this pan is scratched! That will be a challenge..."); Also, try to pay attention to your physical feelings rather than your thoughts and feelings. What is your body feeling?

6   You're welcome to enjoy doing the dishes. First of all, you've already achieved one goal, which is washing the dishes because you want to rather than because you have to. Second of all, why not enjoy yourself? Nice hot water, soap, time to relax...It's almost like taking a bath.

Tip:

Working in the garden or washing the floors can have a similar effect, so if your sink is empty, the floors are always there for you.

2. Mindless Wandering

Who says our will is in our head? Or in our heart? Sometimes it's our feet that know what they want.

Ingredients:

Nothing

Directions:

1 Go out for a walk.

2 Don't decide where you're going. You're not trying to get anywhere.

3 Try to take lesser-known paths, and if you're in a place you know well — try to walk around as if you're a tourist, seeing it for the first time.

4 Don't forget that you are wandering. **Your walk has no purpose, and you can slow down.**

5 Try to let your feet lead the way. Let them decide where you're going. Try to keep your thoughts out of the process. If you reach a crossroads and you wonder which way to turn — take the path that appeals to you most, even if there's no rational explanation for your choice.

6 If a clear desire arises, like stopping, or sitting, or buying something to eat — allow yourself to follow your desire. You have time, you have no goal, so why not do what you want?

7 Don't be tempted to cut your walk short. Walk for at least 20 minutes, and don't hesitate to stay out for three hours either.

Tip:

Wander with your phone turned off. Silencing or muting it isn't enough. Resist the temptation to check if anyone needs you. The phone is great for knowing what other people want from you but you won't find what you want there at all.

3. A Glass of Decaffeinated Water

"Wait, do I really want coffee? Maybe I want tea? Or is it an apple?"

Ingredients:

A glass of water

Directions:

1 Drink a glass of water.

2 After the glass of water you might have a clearer understanding of what it was you wanted to put in your mouth. If one glass doesn't help, have another.

Tip:

This recipe is recommended for people who drink a lot of coffee. Try to replace another cup of coffee for a glass of water. **You might find that it wasn't coffee you wanted, but something else.** Maybe something like a short break that even a glass of decaffeinated water can provide.

4. Media Cleanse

It's hard to listen to yourself if you're listening to the news.

Ingredients:

An Off button

Directions:

1 Turn it all off. Turn off the television, the speakers, the media sites on the computer, all social media and streaming, turn off the car radio. Turn it all off.

2 Consume no media for a week: no social media, no papers or magazines, no radio, no podcasts. Don't watch series, nor movies, nor sports.

3 What's left? You can listen to music you choose or read a book. You can go to the movies, a concert or a play, even to a football game.

4 Once a day, for one minute, you can go online and read the news. If something truly important happened it would be in the headlines.

5 Don't worry. **The silence around you will only seem threatening at first.** Soon enough you'll find it quite friendly.

6 After your cleanse, begin consuming media gradually:

7 Go back to using only what you want to see or hear.

Every time you reach for the On button ask yourself: Do you really want to watch minor league football? Do you really want to watch another episode? Or are you watching that episode because you don't know what it is you want?

8   Try to start with content which is neither social media nor current affairs, for example, a radio station which plays music without excessive talk.

9   Opt for movies over series, and short series (single season, 8 episodes at most) over long addictive series.

10 Prefer magazines and Sunday editions over the daily news.

Tip:

The Idea is to change your media consumption habits, so that they are in line with your desires and free up quiet time to hear yourself. It's hard to hear our will when the media is blaring.

If the idea of a full media cleanse worries you — start with a "media diet": Avoid the consumption of news and current affairs (or social media if that's your thing) on all media platforms. You can read the news (or check your social media apps) once a day. Remember, following your current self is much more relevant than following current affairs.

5. Tasks in the Oven

Can be done metaphorically but is best done physically.

Ingredients:

List of tasks

Oven set at 0 degrees

Directions:

1 Collect all your tasks, to-do lists and chores, those you meant to do today and those you meant to do during the week.

2 Write them all down so that you don't forget any of them.

3 Open the oven and place the list inside.

4 Set the timer for two hours. **During this time, you can't do any of your tasks. They are all in the oven.**

5 If you remember other tasks while you're waiting, write them down and put them in the oven too.

6 I recommend adding any constructive plans of action that arise at this time to the oven. Thoughts of spontaneously cleaning the house, checking your bank balance, working in the yard, buying tickets to a juggling festival or scheduling blood tests should all be condemned to the oven.

7 If your mind starts saying things like "But I have to…" or even "I really want to do the laundry," excuse yourself by saying "Sorry, but those tasks are in the oven right now, and will be there for at least two hours."

8 While your tasks are in the oven — you can do whatever you want. Even if you don't know what you want to do (which is completely normal) — leave all of your tasks in the oven, because if you take them out they will fill up your time and leave no space for your true desires to emerge.

Tip:

If you truly believe you have a task so important it can't go in the oven, remind yourself that you are not the Chief of Staff. If you have the time to read this recipe all the way through (including the tip!) you probably don't have any tasks that can't wait for a couple of hours.

6. Ten Extra Minutes

Adding 10 extra minutes between one task and the next can make a huge difference.

Ingredients:

Advanced planning

Directions:

1 Add 10 extra minutes to everything on your schedule: 10 extra minutes for getting ready in the morning, 10 extra minutes for the commute, 10 extra minutes before or after the meeting, 10 extra minutes between shopping and running errands.

2 What do you do with these 10 extra minutes? You take them to stop and recall: What did I want? From this day? From this meeting? How did I want to get organized this morning? Which desires are motivating me to run these errands?

3 If you have an extra moment after stopping and recalling, use it for something purposeless, like gazing at the sky for a few minutes. Praise yourself for successfully finding time to gaze at the sky on such a busy day.

Tip:

Western culture teaches us to be effective. This efficiency permits a great deal of *doing*, but very little *being*. Most of us suffer from a chronic lack of *"being"* time, and without *"being"* there can be no *"well-being"*.

7. Stop and Look Back

It doesn't just sound strange, it looks strange too.

Ingredients:

Readiness to look strange

Directions:

Every time you feel you have no time for yourself because someone needs you, wants something, pressures you; Every time you feel the stress mounting, the tasks piling up, time running out; Every time your pace quickens, your pulse races, your breath shortens:

1. Stop. Physically stop what you're doing. If you're walking down the street — stop walking. If you're typing — stop typing. If you're driving — Pull over. If you're thinking — calm your thoughts.

2. Look back. Physically turn your head, look back and see: **There is no one chasing you.**

3. Take a deep breath and keep going, a little bit slower, because there's no one chasing you.

4. Stopping mid-flight goes against our primal instincts. That is surely the difference between man and beast: We don't have to act solely upon our instincts.

Now, when you are no longer instinctively fleeing, ask yourself calmly: What do *I* want to do now? Do I want to do this task which stresses me out? Perhaps another task? Or maybe I want to take a moment before continuing?

Tip:

Instead of coming to a complete stop you can go into slow motion. Artificially slow your physical actions down: Walk. Slower. Type. Slower. Drive. Slower. Reach. For. The. Phone. In. Slow. Motion. It doesn't need to be drastic or odd. Even a reduction of 20 percent will do the trick.

8. Worry Neutralizing Chai Masala

Worries are the greatest enemy of our free will, and this is the way to neutralize them.

Ingredients:

A glass of Chai Masala

Directions:

1 Make yourself a glass of Chai Masala, or anything else that reminds you of India. You can light incense or put on some Indian music.

2 Make a list of all your current worries. Worries at work, concerns about the family, financial worries, health issues, concerns for your country, getting the dishwasher fixed…. Everything. Anything on your mind and disturbing your equanimity.

3 Next to every concern, write an appropriate first step to take in order to solve the issue, and when you want to do it (maybe today, maybe tomorrow, maybe later in the week…)

4 If there is no concrete action to take — write "No available action."

5 You have just made a list of concerns and a list of actions to take and when to take them, or have understood that there is no action you can take. **Now you have no need to worry, as there is nothing to worry**

about; Either you have worries and you know what you need to do – so there's nothing to worry about; Or you have worries with no available plan of action, so there is little point in worrying about them.

6 Neutralizing your concerns will allow your will, which has been buried deep in the caverns of your subconsciousness (who would dare to want something when there is so much to worry about?) — to emerge. Sit back, relax, take a sip of your Chai Masala, and let those desires reveal themselves.

7 Why India? Just look up "Then Why Worry" on YouTube. I highly recommend it!

Tip:

Don't fret...your worries will return. We are all a little addicted to worrying. Sometimes we prefer dealing with our concerns rather than discovering our desires. Consistency and practice will go a long way to reduce our worries, so repeat this recipe regularly.

9. Sitting

Dare I say "mindfulness" or "meditation"....

Ingredients:

A comfortable place to sit

A timer

Directions:

1 Sit comfortably. There is no need to sit on the floor in a lotus position. You're not a monk. You can sit on a chair or on the couch, just make sure you're not slouching.

2 Set the timer for 20 minutes.

3 Close your eyes.

4 Pay attention to what is happening here and now. What are you paying attention to? Perhaps you're aware of your breathing. Perhaps you notice your posture. Maybe you hear noises outside. Maybe you feel physical feelings. Thoughts arise and thoughts drift through your head. Your "here and now" is always changing. Pay attention to what is happening right now.

5 **Don't try to do anything. There's no need.** Don't try to control your feelings or calm your thoughts. Don't try to "succeed". There is no right or wrong. Nothing to do, nowhere to go, no one to be.

6 You might find that amongst all the "here and now" moments a desire arises. It might be an urge to do something right away. It might be a more meaningful desire emerging from the depths of your will. One way or another, there's no need to act immediately. Write your desire down and continue sitting for the rest of the session.

7 When the timer rings, turn it off. Take a moment before opening your eyes. Recall any desires that emerged. Take another moment before returning to your daily life and ask yourself, "What do I want *now? Now*, after 20 minutes of sitting, what do I *want?*"

Tip:

Look for mindfulness instructions on youtube, put on your earphones and sit.

10. Get Out of Bed and Out of the House

Perfect for those mornings when you feel there's nothing you want and nothing to get out of bed for.

Ingredients:

Comfortable walking shoes

Directions:

Your free will needs to wake up just as much as you do. A sleepy will might seem nonexistent, but it is nevertheless there, so:

1. Get out of bed.
2. Get dressed, brush your teeth, have something to drink, and immediately leave the house.
3. Take a brisk 10-minute walk. Head back home. You can try to run or skip too.
4. **Now that your will is awake, there's someone to talk to.** Ask yourself what you want.

Tip:

Try preparing for the next day the night before. Think about tomorrow and remind yourself of the good things you would like to get done in the upcoming day. This may help you get up and going in the morning.

11. Fog Lights

As Dr. Seuss said in "Oh, The Places You'll Go!": "Except when you don't. Because sometimes you won't."

Ingredients:

A little bit of faith

Directions:

Sometimes nothing helps. None of the recipes work, everything seems pointless and bland, and you don't have an inkling of what it is you want. What can you do?

1. Understand that you're in a fog.

2. Behave as you would when driving in fog:

    a. Slow down: Don't do anything rash. Don't make any important decisions. Don't try to muscle through the hard times. Stick to your routine.

    b. Turn on your fog lights: Let those around you know you're not at your best and that they should keep their distance.

    c. Advance slowly and carefully: Don't pull over. Try to keep moving — both externally and internally. This will help you get out of the fog.

3. Remember: The fog, by nature, will dissipate. Everything shifts, changes and passes. Even if you are stuck

and disoriented — good winds will eventually scatter the fog and clarity will return.

Tip:

I wrote this recipe after coming out of a three- or four-day fog. It was only when I was out that I remembered, for the umpteenth time, that I didn't need to work so hard at getting out of the fog since it was almost always useless. The fog scattered despite my efforts. In the book of Exodus, God is in the smoke and clouds on Mt. Sinai And Moses walks straight into this fog to meet Him. Sometimes the fog is there for a good purpose.

Remember: 1) The fog serves a purpose. 2) Any attempt to get out may be futile. 3) If you insist on making an effort while in the fog, you might as well use that energy to hang up the shelves you promised to hang long ago.

12. Today I'm a Prince

Today I'm a Prince so I'm writing this recipe in verse.

I'm a prince and I can do whatever I want.

The Kingless Kingdom will get by,
the Knightess Princesses will save themselves,
The food will be served by another man,
and finances... Well, who cares about finances today?!

Today I'm A Prince.
Let the desert be served!

The poet's intent is to show that we play many roles in our lives — King, knight in shining armor, servant, Minister of Finance.... **Today you may choose the role that has no commitments and carries no responsibilities.** Choose to be the prince who enjoys life and does as he pleases.

PART II:
NEW REVELATIONS

Recipes that Reveal New Desires

We are awash with habits: daily habits, thought patterns, the ways in which we choose to consume…all a blessing, because otherwise it would be hard to function. But to reveal new desires we need to leave our habitual comfort zone behind. The recipes in this section will help our consciousness take a journey to mostly enjoyable and surprising new areas, where we will discover all sorts of hidden desires.

13. First Time

When was the last time you did something for the first time?

Ingredients:

A bit of curiosity

A dash of daring

Something to write on

Directions:

1. Do something for the first time.

2. What should it be? It's really not that important: You can take yourself out to a Philharmonic concert (if you've never been), or take yourself into the kitchen and prepare Tiramisu (if you've never made it) or sign up for a ballet class (if you've never worn tights in public). The point is to do something you've never done before, so that you may have a new experience.

3. There are so many things you've never done. You should make a list: Big things, small things, easy things, things you wouldn't be caught dead doing…. Don't hesitate to write them all down. Give it at least 20 minutes, and keep the list open for ideas that may come up over the next few days.

4. Don't limit your list to things you want to do since that might be too short…. **The drive to do something**

for the first time doesn't have to be fueled by desire. Curiosity will suffice. A bit of curiosity will help your list encompass things you would never dream of wanting ("I wonder what chest hair removal would feel like...").

5 Now, add a dash of daring as needed, and choose something on your list to do today, for the very first time!

Tip:

Usually we want something, then we do it. But if we don't know what we want, doing something first can give us a new experience, something outside of our known boundaries. It is out there we might discover a new desire.

14. The Other Alternative

Shimon Peres once said: "If you have to make an important decision and you have two options, and only two options — look for the third option."

Ingredients:

Two bad Options

Directions:

If reality gives you two bad options (for example: driving your daughter to soccer practice thus arriving at the garage too late to pick up your car; Or picking up your car on time and disappointing your daughter who will miss her practice) — How will you do what you want?

1. Avoid both options.

2. Look for a third option.

3. There is always a third, and better, option. **Just because you don't see it doesn't mean it isn't there.** How do we know that's true? Because children are the most creative creatures on the planet, and they always find a third option they want. And because Shimon Says.

4. The third option can be something completely new, or it can be a new way of breaking up the tasks and choos-

ing certain parts. Perhaps it can be a different combination of both options. If nothing else works, you can always ask a friend for help, and give him two options: Either drive your daughter to soccer practice or pick up your car.

Tip:

Think like a child.

15. Going Out with a Friend

Out with a friend, not with the gang.

Ingredients:

A friend

Directions:

1 Make a list of close friends.

2 Make sure you're not just picking "the gang". **You're looking for a close friend, someone you can have an intimate conversation with.** Intimate — Not as in "bedroom intimate", but as in a close and personal conversation about yourself and about them, rather than a conversation about politics or money.

3 Try to make your list varied. Look beyond the regular two or three friends you would naturally choose. Maybe someone from the past, a childhood friend, a neighbor you appreciate, or someone from work you've always been curious about.

4 Aim for a heterogenous list, containing a variety of people of different ages and backgrounds.

5 Now, choose someone off your list and make a date with them. Just the two of you, no other people allowed.

6 Talk about your life. Even a conversation about politics can easily become a conversation about your hopes and

dreams, your preferences, your challenges, your desires and how to know what you want…

7 Make sure to set aside at least two hours for these dates, and schedule them once a month, with a variety of friends. Each and every one of them will help you see life, yourself and your desires from a fresh and different angle.

Tip:

It may feel strange and awkward to invite a friend on a date. You can always say you would like to meet for some advice. People love to give advice and your friend will be happy to join you.

16. Coincidental conversations

My desire to write this book was the result of a coincidental conversation in line for coffee. It works!

Ingredients:

A coincidence

Directions:

1 If you chance upon the opportunity to have a coincidental conversation — Don't miss it. Someone says something Intriguing. Even asks a question? **Instead of giving a laconic answer or a polite smile, engage in conversation.**

2 How does one engage in conversation? First and foremost, show interest. Show interest in the person who is coincidentally in line behind you at the supermarket. Ask them where they live (...West of town?... What's that like?), what do they do for a living (...just starting a second career?), and how is that frozen pie in his cart? Does he recommend it?

3 Don't force yourself on the other person, nor force the conversation to be about your desires. The fact that you want to help yourself know what you want is not his problem. But you can still discover a path to your desires with the help of others. Everyone you meet holds a clue to your will, whether it's moving to a better neighborhood, starting a fresh career, or eating a tastier pie.

Tip:

Try to engage in conversation with people who are less coincidental too. If you meet an old acquaintance, ask him how he is and mean it. If you ask sincerely, you might get an answer rich in clues and suggestions, not just the regular "fine, and you?". And if someone asks you how you are, treat them to a richer answer too. Your answer will hold clues for them and for yourself.

17. Unfamiliar music

Instead of Rock, try Baroque.

Ingredients:

Streaming music app

Directions:

1 Play a playlist of an unknown genre of music or an unknown artist (like James McAlister. Have you ever heard of James McAlister?!)

2 You can listen to the music attentively, or play it in the background, loud enough to hear, while you do other things.

3 Let the playlist play for at least 30-40 minutes.

4 Although you're in familiar surroundings, your brain, upon hearing the unfamiliar music, will take your thoughts and feelings to unfamiliar places. Your Self is affected by the unfamiliar sounds in a "homeopathic" manner. **The musical unknown attracts other unknowns, and amongst them you have a good chance of finding new and unknown wishes and desires.**

5 Listen to the music for a few days in a row, until it feels familiar. Then it's time for a new genre.

Tip:

This recipe works well with other things too, not just music. Try clothing (dress in a new style), food (eat differently), even the way you walk (yes, walk differently for a few days), and you might discover new desires.

18. A Couple of Hours by the Sea

Two hours of aimless gazing will most probably produce an extraordinary moment of clarity.

Ingredients:

A comfortable place to sit

Directions:

1 Go to the beach alone.

2 Find a comfortable place to sit.

3 Stare at the sea.

4 Don't try to do anything. Quite the opposite, try to do nothing.

5 You can bring a journal for jotting down your thoughts, but avoid distractions like a newspaper or a book, and ignore the phone.

6 Let the sea and the repetitiveness of the waves clear your mind of thoughts and worries. This can take some time. As in the law of communicating vessels, the moment your mind clears it will have space for new ideas and emerging desires.

7 When is it time to leave? **Notice the moment when you've had enough and are filled with the desire to get up and go.** If it's because you remem-

bered something you need to do, it's not time yet. But if you are filled with a sense of purpose and drive, or even a calm sense of freedom and space — the time has come.

Tip:

It doesn't have to be two hours, nor does it have to be facing the sea, but it should be a relaxing and preferably natural setting.

19. Total Boredom

Are you bored? Perfect! It means you're about to discover a new desire.

Ingredients:

Zero distractions

Directions:

1 Create a space with zero distractions. Turn off all media and get rid of your Smartphone. Remove anything that might distract you.

2 Avoid eating and drinking, including coffee and snacks. You can have a glass of water.

3 Avoid doing any mundane tasks, even meditating.

4 Be bored: Do nothing, then do nothing, then repeat.

5 Keep being bored, patiently. Your boredom will increase.

6 Just as your boredom increases, it will suddenly pass. It will be instantaneous. Pay attention to this moment, because this is the moment a new interest will manifest. You will suddenly want to do something.

7 **Mind that your new interest is indeed new and not a tricky distraction trying to gain your attention.** Don't despair, your boredom will always pass and new desires will be revealed.

Tip:

Boredom Bites: If you suddenly find yourself bored midday, for instance, while you're waiting for your daughter to end class and it's taking longer than the two minutes she promised it would take — Avoid your phone and utilize your time to get properly bored. New desires can arise in even a short moment of boredom.

20. What Don't I Want?

You don't know what you want but you know what you don't? Great start!

Ingredients:

Pen and Paper (or a Keyboard and Screen)

Directions:

1 Make a list of everything you know you don't want in your life anymore. Big things and small things. For example: I don't want to work under pressure. I don't want to walk the dog. I don't want pea soup. I don't want to get angry as much as I do. I don't want to sleep on the left side of the bed. I don't want dirty socks in the living room….

2 Sort the list into two categories: Things that are easy to achieve and things that are harder to pull off.

3 Further sort each category into two secondary categories: Things that are solely dependent on me, and those I need others' cooperation to attain.

4 Begin with the easy to achieve things that solely depend on your actions. **Now that you know what you don't want, it's easier to recognize what you do want:** You want to make tomato soup instead of pea soup. You want to collect the dirty socks in the living room….

5. Move on to the easy things that require cooperation from others. Clearly state your desires and your difficulties in compromising your needs to those involved.

6. Sometimes a clear, heartfelt statement of intent will do the job. Sometimes it takes more work to find a solution acceptable by all. And yes, sometimes you will do things you don't want, because you would rather have a happy partner than sleep on the right side of the bed.

Tip:

Put the list of hard to achieve things aside for the moment. You can try other recipes that might help you with some, but it's also fine to leave them for another day, week, or even month. The fact that you've written them down is a great achievement in and of itself. By stating what you don't want to yourself, you've opened the door to things you want, and those desires are now cooking on the back burners of your mind. They will emerge, ready and waiting, in the fullness of time.

21. While You Were Angry

Something dissatisfying happened. Don't blame anybody.

Ingredients:

Something dissatisfying that happened

Directions:

1 Parking tickets, noisy neighbors, sudden rain… Don't blame a soul! Give yourself a moment before you get angry. If you get angry or place blame on others, you're missing an opportunity to learn something new about yourself.

2 The way you feel about things is in your hands: Who says you need to get upset when you get a ticket? The Dalai Lama would probably laugh. Mahatma Gandhi would smile at the sound of noisy neighbors. Gene Kelly would dance in the rain. All of these are proof that there is always another reaction possible in every unpleasant situation.

3 After laughing and smiling and dancing (or just plain getting angry) — be grateful, because **when something annoying happens, it helps you realize that you clearly want the opposite:** A solution for your parking problem. A conversation with your neighbor about the time he works on his Harley. An umbrella.

Tip:

"Don't blame anyone" includes not blaming yourself. No matter what you did, you were doing your best. Next time, try to improve, and get those vegetables out of the oven before they turn into charcoal.

22. Aspire like the One You Admire

You don't know what you want, but if you were someone else — What would *he* want?

Ingredients:

Imagination to soar on

Directions:

1 Choose somebody you admire. Admire = appreciate the way he leads his life. Someone you believe lives well, knows how to live life. Someone you would want to be like.

2 It doesn't have to be someone specific. It can be a fictional character you admire, the person you would want to be or the best version of yourself.

3 Imagine you're that person, or that he is now in your shoes, with your set of circumstances, your limitations, and your options. What would *he* want if he were in your place?

4 Allow yourself to fully inhabit his character. Let your imagination soar. Let his will rise and his desires come forth. Don't stop with his first desire. Let all his other desires arise as well.

5 You may find that some of these desires are bizarre, fantastic and impossible to attain. That's ok, there's no need to realize these desires. **Have no fear. You**

can imagine anything you want. These are "his" desires, not yours, and he can want anything he pleases.

6 Return to reality's port. Open your heart and ask yourself: Which of "his" desires would you happily make your own?

Tip:

Sometimes we don't know what we want because our desires frighten us. Why are we afraid? Because we fear we might not succeed in realizing our will and suffer disappointment, even failure. Maybe our desires have the potential of shaking the foundations of everything that is known and safe in our life or can hurt the people we love. These are frightening prospects, and in an act of defense, we might not even allow ourselves to experience our sense of desire or realize it exists.

This recipe can help us experience our will safely and gently, in the guise of another person rather than in ourselves.

23. Poor Man, Rich Man

If life hasn't taken you to financial extremes, this recipe will.

Ingredients:

A bank account. Your bank balance is irrelevant.

Directions:

This recipe has two parts. You don't have to do both parts at the same time.

Poor Man

1 Do you know what your monthly average expenses are? If you don't, this is the time to find out. Check your bank account for the last three months, add up all your expenses, and divide the sum by three. That will give you a fairly accurate idea of your monthly expenses.

2 Now — Deduct one quarter of your expenses. Imagine your income has been greatly reduced, or that you have a large unavoidable expense you need to free up money for, and you have no choice but to cut your expenses by 25 percent.

3 Think carefully: What will you give up? Take your time. Don't hurry. Go over all your expenses and check, honestly, what you would give up and what you are not able or willing to do without.

4 The need to give up a quarter of your expenses will force you to examine your desires. You need to reassess your lifestyle, **look at the things you've gotten in the habit of wanting, and checking if these desires are still relevant.** Do these desires still exist, or can they be replaced with other, more relevant ones?

5 This is just an exercise, and a quarter of your expenses is a huge amount. You might be able to fine-tune your desires in significant and surprising ways by cutting just a tenth of your spendings. Even so, try to go all the way and reduce your expenses by a quarter.

6 Now it's time to realize the new and updated desires you discovered! You might even save some money as a bonus.

Rich Man

7 Do you know what your monthly average expenses are? Well, never mind, since they're unimportant. You have just received a huge sum of money by surprise!

8 There is only one condition: You must spend a part of the money within the next year. $400,000 to be precise. You need to spend this money. Not invest it or save it, nor give it to your mom or to your kids.

9 Think carefully: What will you do with the money? What will you spend it on? Take your time. Don't hurry. Imagine this money sitting in your bank account.

Give your thoughts free rein: How would you live if you lived like a millionaire for a year?

10 The need to spend a large sum of money within a year will help you explore your desires and reexamine your habitual "fantasies". Are those fantasies still valid? Or are you able to find new desires, **aspirations your regular self would not even dare to dream of, but your millionaire self can afford.**

11 This is just an exercise, and $400,000 is a lot of money. Even so, try to spend the whole amount. Let your top centile desires reveal themselves.

Tip:

Although this is only an exercise and you don't really possess the "Rich man" funds, examine these desires. Perhaps some of them could be made to come true with less funds than you think? Maybe you can find funding in unexpected places? Try to make them happen, find sources of income that can help you do what you want. You might find that the money you save in the "Poor Man" exercise will do the trick :)

24. Observing a Holy Day. Or Thursday

A secular recipe.

Ingredients:

The ability to stand up for yourself

Directions:

1 Choose a day that you will keep free of obligations. A self-given holiday.

2 Clear this day of all obligations: Work obligations, family obligations, shopping and chores, anything you would consider an obligation.

3 Clear the day of distractions too. This means as little media and social networks as possible.

4 Clear the day of any regular activities you usually do, like your morning run or your evening class.

5 Keep the day clear of all obligations, distractions and routine activities. This is easier said than done. The moment you have a free day it tends to fill up. You'll need to stand up for yourself in the face of pressures both external and internal: "Well, just one meeting…", "I suppose visiting her parents is ok…", or "Nothing wrong with a morning run…"

6 Now that you have a completely clear day, your true desires are free to make an appearance — those desires

that have a hard time revealing themselves in the face of obligations and distractions. Maybe a hike, or a visit to a friend, or a movie at the theater. Perhaps a game of backgammon, or tennis. Anything you want! Your day is free and you can do as you please.

7   If you have a strong desire to have a work meeting, or a run, or even a visit to her parents, do it! Just **make sure it's your free will deciding, and not force of habit, obligation, impulse or compromise**. Telling the difference can be a little tricky, but you can if you try.

Tip:

Even observant people can find keeping a holy day difficult. Be patient with yourself. Remember, any part of the day you manage to keep for yourself is your net gain.

PART III:
EXPLORING THE DEPTHS OF OUR CONSCIOUSNESS

Reinforcing the Foundations of Our Will and Strengthening Desire

We are all born with strong and healthy will power. As we age this muscle weakens, and we strengthen our ability to function effectively and to please others instead. The recipes in this section help us reestablish a strong foundation for our will. We'll train, practice, and improve our ability to perceive our desires clearly and act upon them with ease.

25. Playing Backgammon

Backgammon is a fantastic game for developing life skills, and a little twist makes it perfect for strengthening a faltering will.

Ingredients:

A backgammon board

Basic knowledge of the game

A partner or a backgammon app to play with

Directions:

1 Play a game of backgammon

2 Every time you throw the dice — ask for a number. Yes, every time. Not only when you're desperate and need a double six to save yourself from certain gammon, or a 4-1 to build a point.

3 Make your desires precise. Ask for a specific number for each one of the dice. It's not enough to ask for a "double". Be specific as to which double you want. Nor will asking for "a four" suffice. Make sure you know what you want on both dice.

4 Play at least one game per day, for a period of at least three weeks. Each game has an average of 26 moves, which means exercising your will at least 26 times a day. That's quite a workout!

Tip:

This recipe makes you stop to look at the big picture, decide what your best move is, and ask for it out loud. This is a very different approach than the regular one, where you do your best with what fate deals you, without checking to see what it is you really want.

26. Turning "Need" Into "Want"

Words have power and you want(!) to use them to your benefit.

Ingredients:

Nothing

Directions:

1. Exchange the word "need" for the word "want". Basically, every time you're about to say "I need…", say "I want…"; Every time you think "I have to…", exchange that thought for "I would like to…" or "It would be best to…" For example: I want to pick my daughter up from school. I would like to take my car to the garage. It would be best to do some laundry, I have no socks.

2. If "want" doesn't easily replace "need", try a softer word like "can" or "get to". (I get to take the car to the garage. I can wash the floor today.)

3. Check and see if you really want to do what you think needs doing. If your answer is "Yes" — You're lucky! You just found out you're doing what you want to do and not what you need to do. If your answer is "No" — You have two options:

    a. Postpone everything that needs to be done until a time you want to do it. That way you will either get it done when you want to, or get it done at the last minute (And that is fine. Sometimes the last minute is our will's best friend.)

b. Search your mind for reasons you would want to do something that needs to get done. **Sometimes our desires are hidden under a layer of obligation and can't be seen.** In this case, all we want to do is peel away this layer and discover our true wishes. For instance: "I need to take the car to the garage" can be hiding a desire for a safe and well-functioning car. Seeing things in this light can change both our approach and our actions.

Tip:

Needing to do something doesn't necessarily mean you don't want to do it. Sometimes we genuinely want to do what needs to be done.

27. Keeping a journal

Relax, nobody's going to read it. You don't need to be Hemingway to write it.

Ingredients:

An empty journal (or a lined notebook)

A pen

Directions:

1 Open the journal, take the pen and write something. (there is no replacing the feeling of pen on paper so please don't be tempted to use a keyboard for this recipe).

2 Don't wait for when you have something to write. Write even when you have nothing to say.

3 What should you write about?

   • You can write down the thoughts you're having right now and the feelings you're feeling.

   • You can write what you thought, felt or did yesterday.

   • You can write about what you're hoping will happen tomorrow.

4 Don't censor anything. Nobody will read this, not even you. You're not writing a novel. You're writing for writing's sake. **The writing will help you hear the whispering of your will.**

5 If your writing doesn't flow, try asking yourself a question, then answering it. A good question can be "what do I want to happen today?" and the answer can be a list of things you want to happen, or things you would like to do, or the mood you would like to be in.

6 You can ask other questions like "what makes me happy in life?" or "what good things happened to me yesterday?" Think of yourself as a journalist interviewing yourself: Ask yourself a question and if your Self doesn't answer, try another question.

7 Don't be critical of what you write, don't try to make it good or tidy, witty or smart. The important thing is that you're writing. In this case, quantity is better than quality.

8 Repeat steps 1-7 at least every two or three days and check with yourself when your best time for writing is: Morning? Evening? Maybe on the subway?

Tip:

If you find yourself stuck in front of a blank page, give yourself 20 seconds. You have 20 seconds to write something, anything really, no matter what. Usually, 20 seconds of spontaneous writing will unblock the dam and your writing will flow freely.

28. Taking a Hike

When was the last time you found yourself in nature with a backpack on your back?

Ingredients:

A backpack

Two sandwiches

Two liters of water

Comfortable walking shoes

Directions:

1. Look online and find a hiking trail or nature walk that appeals to you. It should be two or three hours long, circular, and not too far a drive. It shouldn't be too hard either, since you're not looking for a physical challenge.

2. Prepare two sandwiches and place them in your pack along with the water. You can add an apple and a couple of snacks too.

3. Drive to the starting point. Drive slowly and look at the scenery. Your trip has already started.

4. Start hiking. Don't rush. **Your objective is to hike, not to end the trail as quickly as possible.**

5. Walk attentively. Try to divide your attention between four different focal points:

- Your steps. Pay attention to where you are stepping and to your speed. If you speed up or slow down, try to understand why.

- Your surroundings. The natural environment, its sounds, smells and sights.

- Your desires. Are you hungry? Thirsty? Do you want to stop and take a break, rest, or take your bearings?

- Your interests. Notice what interests you, what piques your curiosity. If you're feeling bored, look for something that will interest you. You might find it in nature itself or in the people that walk by, in yourself, your thoughts, and your desires.

6 Take at least one long break, for at least half an hour. Sit in nature, listen to nature, breathe nature, be in nature.

7 When you're done hiking, drive home slowly. Try to stay in hiking mode until you get home.

Tip:

Hike alone.

29. A Month in a Foreign City

Unbelievable? Incredible!

Ingredients:

$5,000-$10,000

Directions:

1 Spend a month in a foreign city

2 Your month could be divided into four different parts:

- First week- Spend it alone.

- Second week — Spend it with your spouse, or with a good friend

- Third and fourth week — Spend it with your children, one at a time for four or five days each. They can share an overlapping day or two if that works for you.

- Spend the last two or three days alone, then go home.

Before you start, there are some preparations to be made:

3 Choose your destination. In and of itself, the destination is not the point. You are the main point of interest, and you'll be interesting no matter where you are. Still, it would be good if the destination fills the following parameters:

- The city should be interesting and welcoming.

- It should be 3 or 4 hours away at most (by plane, train, or car).

- It should be relatively inexpensive, so that financing isn't too big an issue.

4 Learn all you can about the city online. Weather, transportation, restaurants, entertainment, best places to stay.

5 Based on your research, choose an Airbnb rental suitable for a month-long stay (well equipped kitchen, laundry facilities), in a good area (walking distance from points of interest, pleasant and quiet surroundings). It's better to choose an apartment over a hotel since an apartment is both cheaper and more suitable for a long stay.

6 Research all the "must see" attractions in the city. Markets, public buildings, walking tours. These are the things you will **not** do! Feel free to avoid the "musts". You've traveled all this way to find out what you want, not to do what you "must do". You're exempt from seeing the old church. You've seen it online anyways.

After learning the city well, you're ready for the next step: Your inner preparation.

7 Think about your first week alone. Ask yourself "What would I like to experience in New Orleans?" (Or Vancouver, Madrid, or Budapest....) Write down both the question and the answer. Try to imagine what you'll be doing in the city, how you would like to feel, what

activities are fun, how you'll be living and what you'll be going through. (See recipe 27 on keeping a journal for help).

8 Do this every day, for a whole month before your trip. You might find that your answers change over time. The questions can change too. Maybe you'll start asking yourself questions like "what does my ideal day in New Orleans look like?" or "what is my daily schedule like?" Make yourself an ideal daily schedule and write down what happens on a day like that.

You're in a foreign city. What are you going to do alone for a whole week?!

9 This week is like boot camp for the discovery of your will. You have left your routine and your commitments behind. **Nobody here wants anything from you. It's all about what you want.** You can ask "what do I want now?" at any given moment and wait for your response. "I want to rent a bike and ride around." / "Do I really want to eat at that Georgian restaurant tonight? No, I would rather make myself an omelet and some salad." / "Two hours have passed and I'm still enjoying sitting on this bench by the river." / "Now! I want to do my laundry now!" / "How can I be this bored and still not want to see the old church?"

10 You can look back in your journal and see if there is anything you would like to do from your writings. You can choose to do something from there, but only if you want to.

11 What if you're bored?! Well, you will certainly be bored at times, which is great (see recipe 19: Total Boredom). You can ask yourself "why do I find the park boring when I found it interesting a moment ago?" You might find it is not the park that's boring, but you who stopped being interested.

12 Just to be on the safe side, and to ensure your sanity, you should have an "anchor activity". An "anchor activity" is an activity you do daily. Something you know you will do every day and will help you "anchor" your day. It can be a work project, or a creative project like writing or drawing, or maybe studying something you have been wanting to learn, like Quantum Physics. It can be a workshop or a course you take in your foreign city. Guidelines for an "anchor activity" are:

- A continuous activity you can do for no longer than an hour a day.

- Something you like doing, and not be experienced as a burden.

- Something that has no consequences if you choose not to do it.

Manage your expectations for the following weeks.

13 After a week of doing solely what you want, you will meet other desires — those of your spouse or friend. Later you will contend with the desires of your children. To avoid a head on collision of desires you should

prepare ahead for the next few weeks: Ask yourself "How would I like the week with my spouse to be?", "What is an ideal day with my son?"

14 Ask your family members to ask themselves these questions too, and to think of what they desire from a week with you.

15 Look for common desires and find strategies for managing conflicting ones.

16 While you're together make sure you're still listening to your own wishes and desires. This will be challenging with other willful people around you. **It's very important for you to learn how to retain balance between your will and the desires of those around you.**

Preparing to return home

17 Utilize your last few days alone to get back to listening to yourself. Go over the desires you discovered both preparing for the trip and during your stay in the foreign city. See if any of these desires are relevant to your life back home.

18 After your return, give yourself a couple of weeks to readjust. Don't make any intensive plans for this time. Chances are you have come back with several (or many) new desires and aspirations, so give yourself and your surroundings time to get used to the new you.

Tip:

The Idea for this recipe was born when I searched for a 50th birthday present to give myself. It was, indeed, a fantastic gift. There's no need to wait for a "round" birthday though, and it will be great as a 41st birthday gift too.

30. Four Days in the Country

"A Month in a Foreign City" when you only have four days.

Ingredients:

$500-$1,000

Directions:

1 Choose a destination. As in the previous recipe, the destination is not that important, but it will be best if:

 - It's small and has no attractions beyond a grocery store and a pizza place.

 - It's close to nature.

2 After arriving and doing a small orientation walk, ask yourself: "What do I want to do now?" (see points 9-12 in the previous recipe). **It will take you at least a day to slow down and relax, so be patient with yourself.**

3 During these four days do recipe 4: "Media Cleanse", and you might want to combine some "Mindless Wandering" (recipe 2), "Keeping a Journal" (recipe 27), "Taking a Hike" (recipe 28), and if you meet any locals you can try "Coincidental Conversations" (recipe 16).

Tip:

You're in a small place? Stay there. Try to avoid the temptation to hop in the car and look for entertainment elsewhere. Keep your desires within walking distance.

31. Playing Like a Child

Children know what they want. Why not reconnect with your inner child?

Ingredients:

Some silliness

A few partners to play with

Directions:

1 Play a game. Board games, cards, tag, backgammon, checkers, battleship…. Anything you have at home, anything your family enjoys, anything your partners feel like playing.

2 Add some silliness and have some fun. Play, laugh, be immature. Try not to be too competitive or you'll get upset if you lose. Avoid games like chess which tend to be dead serious.

3 Let your inner child, the child you still are, be present in the game. Games offer a haven for playfulness and can legitimize childish behavior. **The more you can reveal your inner child, the more your hidden desires will become apparent.**

Tip:

The best games are played in the backyard. Old fashioned backyard games like tag or "Red light, green light" will get you moving. Full of fun and silliness, they are impossible to play while remaining completely adult.

32. Consciously Listen to Music

Don't just hum along with your playlist, put on a song and really listen to it. You'll be surprised to discover riches you never knew were there.

Ingredients:

A phone and headphones (or a good speaker)

Directions:

1 Choose a song you know and listen to it attentively, with your eyes closed.

2 Try to hear the different layers of the music, those below the melody and lyrics: Listen to the guitar, try to pick out the bassline, pay closer attention to the drums. Maybe you'll be surprised to hear a cello or a clarinet you never noticed before.

3 Don't sing along. Try to ignore the well-known melody. **You are trying to hear things you never heard before, both in the music and in your Self.**

4 Song over? Before you open your eyes and ears to the background noises that get in the way of hearing your Self — give yourself another moment or two to pay attention to the sounds in and around you.

Tip:

This recipe helps us listen to voices we're not accustomed to hearing. By practicing conscious listening of external sounds, we can improve our ability to hear internal sounds, like the calling of our will.

33. Artistic Endeavors

There Is certainly something you can do creatively or perform in an artistic manner.

Ingredients:

An artistic endeavor, soon to be determined.

Directions:

1. Look for an artistic endeavor which is:

   + Neither useful nor effective.

   + Utilizes your emotions more than your mind.

   + Has creative or artistic characteristics, for example: singing, dancing, painting, sculpting, photography, acting, writing poetry, designing textiles, clothing or jewelry.

2. It's fine for your endeavor to have a useful outcome — Like a painting for your living room or improved cardiovascular fitness from dancing — But **your motivation must be creative, not productive.**

3. Engage in your creative activity at least once a week. It's best if you do it daily. Devote yourself your activity and try to lead with your emotions. Give your thoughts a break.

Tip:

Rarely do our desires come from our mind and thoughts. Our desires are hidden in other places, organs we don't usually look at. Sometimes our deepest wishes reside in our heart, our stomach, our hands, even in our legs. This recipe will help us act from there.

34. The Spiritual Path

Buddhism, Kabala, Anthroposophy, Shamanism... All Paths lead to the discovery of your will.

Ingredients:

Curiosity (If you have curiosity, perseverance is practically unnecessary).

Directions:

1. Try. Try a lecture on Shamanism...An Open Day at the Anthroposophy Seminar.... If you don't try, how will you know which spiritual path suits you?

2. Give it a chance. **Don't let cynicism and doubt get in your way.** If you feel the tiniest bit of interest, give it a chance.

3. There is no right way. There is the path that is open to you right now. How will you recognize it? Maybe the path appeals to you: You get a text message offering a new course and it piques your curiosity — Give it a try.

   Perhaps it doesn't pique your curiosity but makes itself magically available! You may not feel terribly attracted to the course, but it seems to be saying: "hey, there's a study group opening up in your neighborhood, on your free evening, no prior knowledge needed, and it's even free..." — Go try it out! You might discover something wonderful.

4 Don't confuse knowledge with a spiritual path. Make sure you didn't sign up for "The history of Buddhism", or "The Foundations of Islam". Knowledge obtained in this manner, as interesting and exciting as it might be, won't help you find your path. In this recipe we're not trying to accumulate knowledge, we're seeking a path to follow. Knowledge and educational achievements, as great as they are, aren't the spiritual guides we're seeking.

Tip:

Your path is individual, and you're not beholden to any one way. Different paths meet, join, cross and converge. I, for instance, started my path with Mindfulness and Buddhism, switched over to Anthroposophy, crossed paths with "The Cosmic University" and added progressive Judaism. I'm quite certain I missed a few interesting turns in the road, and that new paths are right around the bend. I'll try not to miss any of them.

35. Maybe You Should Talk to Someone

There's no easy way to say this. Everybody needs therapy, and that means you do too. Plainly put: You want to get some help.

Ingredients:

Motivation

Directions:

1. Find a therapist. Or a life coach. That's all you need to do.

   Studies show that the most important factor for the success of therapy is the client's motivation (which you have prepared in advance). The second most important factor is the therapist patient relationship. The treatment method has been found to be the least important of the three. So, you don't have to look for a psychologist. **You have to look for a person that can help you,** even if that person is a Biographical Counselor (yes, that's a real thing).

2. How do you find a therapist? The best way is to ask friends for suggestions and recommendations. Ask a friend that lives in your area, so that you can visit your therapist in person, not only via Zoom sessions. If you live near me, I have three warm recommendations:

   a. Tarika Zohar. I met Tarika over a cup of coffee, when I was trying to get her to work with me. During the meeting I realized I was in counseling. Tarika asked me questions that made me notice and reexamine patterns of thought and beliefs that I held (like the belief that prosperity involves a great deal of hard work). I was in counseling with Tarika for three or four years. Tarika employs a method based on the teachings of "The Cosmic University". She opened cards for me, listened to me, explained things, told me about herself, and healed me energetically. I know it sounds "New Age", but Tarika is really grounded. Although I can't explain how it worked, I can wholeheartedly say that I came out of every session feeling wiser and more attuned, and my heart was wider and happier.

b. Amos Avisar. Although I only had two sessions with Amos, I understood that he has something deep and meaningful to offer. Amos employs a method called "Hakomi" in which one is directed to pay attention to one's physical feelings. These sensations can lead to insights, and Amos led our sessions with a great deal of wisdom, sensitivity and empathy. I came out of our two sessions with deeply meaningful and surprising insights.

c. Elisha Wolfin. Elisha employs a method called "Focusing", and although I have never been in treatment with him, we had some deep conversations, and I have enjoyed his weekly lessons on progressive Judaism. Let's say I am waiting for the opportunity to be in therapy with him....

3. Now use the motivation you prepared to help you find a therapist. Try two or three sessions. Decide if you are establishing a good therapist patient relationship. Check your feelings after the session — Do you feel your heart and mind expanding? Check if you're feeling good about yourself after the sessions: Are your meetings helping you not only to understand and forgive yourself, but to love yourself too?

Tip:

It's important that you'll want to go to your meetings. If you feel like they're an obligation or a burden — find a new therapist.

36. Contractions of the Will

This recipe is for when, deep down, you know what you want to do, but your will muscle is so cramped up you almost believe you don't want to do it.

Ingredients:

An issue or situation which tightens you up.

Directions:

Answer the following six questions:

1 "What's the right attitude for this situation?"

   If you could choose the attitude you would be in to get the job done, what would it be? Perhaps you want to feel generous, or curious, or confident. Maybe something else would work better.

2 "What intensity or speed is appropriate for this situation?"

   Do you need to act urgently? Swiftly? Perhaps a relaxed, patient, easy-going approach would be better.

3 "What opportunities does the situation afford?"

   This is the time to remember why you want to do what you want to do. What opportunities are to be had? Perhaps there's a financial opportunity, or the opportunity to do good. Maybe it's an opportunity to feel good about yourself and make yourself happy.

4 "Is there an opportunity for self-development to be had by dealing with the situation?"

Beyond the clear gain in the matter itself, find out what you stand to gain by dealing with your resistance. Perhaps you stand to overcome fear or step out of your comfort zone. Maybe there's an important lesson about yourself to be learned.

5 "What's the first, concrete and responsible step I need to take right now?"

In practical terms, what is it you need to do now? Break the task up into small, concrete steps. Do the next step.

6 "What do I need to do so that I take the next step in the best possible way?"

Right before you take the next step, make sure you've done all of your preparation. Perhaps you need to collect some data, or make sure you have a good attitude, or maybe just take a deep breath.

Now try to have a good attitude(1), adjust your speed(2), remember there's an opportunity to be had(3), and a chance for self-development(4), take the first concrete step(5), and do it all in the best possible way(6).

Here's an example:

I want to invest in real estate, but the thought gives me cramps. I want it to happen, but I don't want to deal with it.

1 "What's the right attitude for this situation?"

   I would like to have an attitude of curiosity, to feel like I am discovering a new interest and finding pleasure in it.

2 "What intensity or speed is appropriate for this situation?"

   I want to be relaxed. I don't want to feel pressured to act, even if my investment money waits a while.

3 "What opportunities does this situation afford?"

   There is a financial opportunity here that may afford me financial well-being and a sense of freedom.

4 "Is there an opportunity for self-development to be had by dealing with the situation?"

   The situation will force me to grow, to explore new territories outside of my comfort zone, and to develop a healthier attitude to wealth and prosperity.

5 "What's the first, concrete and responsible step I need to take right now?"

   I need to set up a meeting with a real-estate consultant.

6 "What do I need to do so that I take the next step in the best possible way?"

In preparation for the meeting, I need to go over my calculations. I also need to take a deep breath and cultivate a joyful attitude. I'm going to take care of my family's financial well-being; how can I not be joyful?

Tip:

For your first project, choose something that tightens you up, not something that paralyzes you.

37. Desire Under Investigation

Sometimes doubt can creep up on budding desires: Maybe my desire is fake? Misleading? Maybe I don't really want what I want? This is a recipe for advanced will makers.

Ingredients:

An able investigator

An honest subject

Directions:

1. A desire arises. That's great. Examine it: Why do you want this? Is there a hidden motive? **What is the desire beneath the desire?** Perhaps your desire is superficial and there's a deeper, authentic motive lying below the surface. For example:

   + I want to pay for my car registration. Why? Because I have to? So that I'm busy rather than bored? To feel useful? These motives have no real benefit. I don't want to do things because I have to, or because I don't want to deal with boredom, or because I need to feel useful. So no, I don't want to pay for my car registration. Not right now.

   + I want to call my friend. Why? Because I need a distraction from my thoughts and worries? Because I have to return the call to avoid unpleasantness? Neither are beneficial motives. I guess I don't want to call my friend right now.

- I want to go to the beach. Why? So that I'm in an environment which will help me hear myself? That's a good motive. I really want to go to the beach. But if my motive is to avoid confrontation at home — I don't really want to go to the beach.

- I want to walk the dog. Really? Yes, I really want to walk the dog. I want to get out, move around, get some exercise. I really want to walk the dog! Although I have to walk the dog, I also have a beneficial motive.

- I want to call my friend again. Why? Because I want to tell him what's been happening with me and benefit from his point of view and insights. I also want to hear about what is happening with him and learn from his point of view and insights, and help him with my point of view and insights. These are good and beneficial motives. I really want to call my friend now.

Tip:

Sometimes we have strange desires. Really strange desires. So strange that it's even embarrassing to give an example. These desires are worth investigating too. Not because they might be fraudulent, but because they might be truthful. Before you say, "I must be losing my mind", check what might be normal about your desire. Does it hide a legitimate need? A kernel of truth? There may be a true and just desire hiding in that moment of insanity.

38. Kicking the Cheese

Before the catastrophe that changes your life happens and helps you to realize what you wanted all along; Before the Universe, G-d and Fate move your cheese...I invite you to kick it away yourself.

Ingredients:

A brave heart, desperation, or a crystal-clear understanding that "I don't want to live like this anymore."

Directions:

1 Kick the cheese. Don't just move it, kick it hard and far. In real terms, change your lifestyle drastically.

2 What kind of change should you make?

   Some people might quit their excellent jobs and spend a few months unemployed. Some people might choose to pursue an old dream and make it come true. Some will go to India for six months, with or without their families. I know somebody who was extremely good at what he did and chose to become a bus driver for two years. Another acquaintance had a profession which took 7 years of study, and one day he decided to leave it all and become a mosaic artist. Another friend, also extremely good in his field, chose to work in a coffee shop twice a week, behind the counter, smiling and asking: "Would you like this to go?"

3. How will you know you are really kicking the cheese and not just moving it around? Because the change you make will be:

- Something extraordinary that few people do.

- Something that will be hard to talk about because people will be critical of your actions

- Something that goes against common sense, the opposite of everything we're engineered to think and desire and might also be a financial risk.

- **Something scary, or exhilarating, or both.**

4. From here — you're on your own. After you understand that you have to kick your cheese far and wide, and you know how you're going to do it — you are in the hands of fate. And fate — is in your hands! How exciting is that!

Tip:

I ended up taking a year off. One day, while I was writing in my journal (see recipe 27) and preparing for a month in a foreign city (see recipe 30), I understood that "I don't want to live like this anymore". "Like this" was referring to the burden of earning our livelihood. I understood that the burden of "breadwinner" was suppressing my will and my desire, clouding my ability to find new interests and direction. I asked my spouse if she would be willing to allocate a part of our savings for me to be able to take a year off. She was. I'm grateful for every moment and every day of that year, and I don't regret even one penny spent on myself and my wellbeing.

39. Equalizing Identities

This recipe looks at "what do I want" from a fresh angle: Who is the "I" who wants what it wants?

Ingredients:

4-5 identities or roles in life

Directions:

We all have various roles we play in life. We are parents, spouses, children, careerists, friends, lovers, activists, poets…and we try to hold these roles in a delicate balance, a balance in which no role overshadows the other. Sometimes there's an imbalance among the different roles, and while one identity's wishes and desires are loud and clear, other voices are pushed aside.

This recipe invites you to play with an "identity equalizer", on which you will be able to turn up the volume of different identities and hear what they really want.

How is it done?

1 Make a list of all your identities or roles that you play in life.

   In and of itself, this is an interesting exercise: How do you define yourself? What different parts make up your "Self"? Try to rate these different roles according to the importance or "volume" they have in your life. You may learn something interesting about yourself.

2. Choose one role and, for one week, raise its volume and dominance in your daily life. **Try to be this identity in the best way possible.** There is no need to completely silence your other identities, but let this one take the lead for the whole week.

   I, for example, took the role of "Father" and amped it up for a week. (this is the place to give credit to my daughter, who came up with this recipe, with the desire to receive some quality "father time"). Each day I reminded myself that today I am a father first and foremost, and would ask myself: How can I express my best fatherhood today? How can I be the best version of father I am able to be?

   The results were both surprising and joyful: Things I thought of as a "pain" (Daddy, drive me…) became easy and fun, and I even volunteered for some without needing to be asked; My daughters' presence was no longer annoying. Quite the opposite, spending time with them was extremely pleasurable; I gave them my attention generously and gladly; I bought my daughter a surprise gift for (I am embarrassed to admit) the very first time and was awarded with a tremendously satisfying "Who got me this? You are now my favorite person on earth!" shout from the next room.

3. After a week, change your leading role. Choose a different identity from your list and crank up the volume. You can choose an identity that normally has a big presence in your life and make it even louder.

I did this with the "careerist". Here too, I had interesting insights, although not always pleasant. I discovered aspects of my career I wasn't happy with. I also discovered aspects of my career which I enjoy very much. In general, I learned that I would like to lower the volume on the role of "careerist" in my life.

4   Thus, week after week, for 4-5 weeks (or even longer), choose an identity and raise its volume.

5   At the end of each week summarize the things you have learned: What understanding would you like to incorporate into your life? What would you happily do without? What volume would you like to give this identity in the "I" that you are?

Tip:

Perhaps you'll choose an identity, only to find out that you are unable to raise its volume. Maybe it's hard to be "better" at what you're doing, or to express yourself in a new and different way. What does it mean? It can be one of three things: Maybe you have the volume "just right" and there's no need for change. Maybe this identity is not really yours anymore and should be given up. Or — And this is the most interesting option — this identity is asking for a completely different course of action. You have a field of new desires and possibilities for self-expression waiting to be plowed and cultivated.

40. Ask "What do I Want?"

Keep asking, even if you don't get an answer.

Ingredients:

Pen and notebook or journal

Directions:

1. Every morning ask yourself "What do I want today"?

2. Add spontaneous "What do I want?" questions throughout the day. You can expand and revise the question as well. Try "What do I want to happen?", "How do I want to feel?", "What do I want to do?", "Where do I want to be?" or other, similar, questions.

3. Write down all of your answers in your notebook or journal. Don't censor yourself, no matter how silly or fantastical your answers might be.

4. **Even if the answers don't come immediately — stay with the question for 5 minutes.** If you still don't have an answer, let the question go.

5. Do this for a month. At the end of the month, sum things up:

   - Go through your journal, read and recall your desires and ask yourself — nonjudgmentally — if any of these desires are still relevant, and if any of them have become a reality.

- Ask yourself: "What do I want for the next month?". Write it down.

- Ask yourself: "What do I want for the next year?". Write it down.

6 As the days go by, you'll find that the answers come more freely, and your ability to know what you want will improve. That's why keeping it up for a month is so beneficial, persevering for two months is great, and getting into a habit of daily questioning for the years to come is better than best.

Tip:

Night work: Before you go to sleep, try to reconstruct your day. (This is best done backwards, starting from a moment ago until what you did in the morning). After your reconstruction is done, and right before you fall asleep, ask yourself "What do I want?". Don't try to answer the question, just send it into the night. In the morning, recollect your dreams. Perhaps you'll receive a hint or an answer. Do this every night for a week, or until you achieve clarity, whichever comes first.

HINTS

Five Hints for the Question "What Do I Want?"

Hint No. 1: I Want to Live

We all want to live. But as a wise man once said: "Just because you're breathing, doesn't mean you're alive." What does "being alive" mean to you?

Is this too big a question? Maybe it's easier to look at others, rather than at yourself. Look at the people you say are "really living", or "know how to live". What is it they're doing that you're not?

I, for example, look at my friend Hagit. She's my "knows how to live" person. I realize that what I translate as "knowing how to live" is her ability to allow herself both the large and small things she desires. She keeps herself at the top of her priority list and is rarely stingy with herself. For someone like me, with a tendency to asceticism, this is what "really living" means. I understand that overcoming my asceticism is something I would like to do. Since I want to be more like Hagit, I bought myself an espresso maker.

But you don't want to stop at the espresso maker. **When I ask myself what "really living" is for me, I discover more and more clues to what it is I desire.** I don't ask myself per se. I start the sentence and myself completes it:

Me: Really living is…

Myself: …being creative.

Me: Wow, thanks, Great hint. I want to be creative. Maybe I'll try to write a song today…

Me: Really living is…

Myself: …having a variety of experiences.

Me: OK… I want a variety of experiences, something new. I've never been to the Opera…let's try that.

Me: Really living is…

Myself: …being in motion.

Me: Well…That's a little deeper, but I think I know what it means. I want to reach new places, both inside and out. Not to freeze in place, not get too used to my comfort zone. To be constantly developing.

It's harder to translate this desire into concrete steps, but it's comforting in and of itself: When I'm going through hard times (externally or internally) I can remind myself that I'm in motion, and I can make sure to remain in motion until this hard patch becomes a part of my past. When I'm in a good patch and feeling great, I again remind myself that I'm in motion and I make sure to stay in motion rather than get stuck in a good place. Being in motion is what I truly want.

It's your turn now. What does "being alive" mean to you?

Hint No. 2: I want to Be Free

Everybody wants to be free; nobody ever really is. We are all slaves to something, on an eternal Exodus. But the will to be free can serve as a strong indicator for concrete wishes, which can be derived from this basic desire.

If I desire to be free, I need to pay attention to the places where I am not free. I need to recognize the times in which I feel limited, and situations in which I feel bound. What blocks me. When do I feel like a slave, and what am I a slave to?

For instance: Other people's desires — limit me. Obligations I have taken upon myself — Bind me. Social conventions — block me. And, of course, money. I'm a slave to making a living.

Money is a good place to start. If money restricts my freedom — what concrete desires can I derive?

The obvious one is that I want more money! That is, of course, a worthy first derivative. We all want more money. But it's not the only desire to be had. **This is where it gets interesting, because there are other desires hidden under the obvious ones.**

For example:

I might want to work less for my money, because what really binds me is the time and effort I must invest to make it, rather than the actual amount I have. It's the loss of time and energy that makes me feel like a slave.

Maybe it's not effort, but fear that binds me. If there are things I want but am afraid to obtain because they're too expensive, I might need to rethink my priorities and allocate my funds differently. Perhaps my desires are not set in the right order.

Or maybe I just want to revise my attitude towards money, to make money and property less central. To be less preoccupied with financial issues and stop worrying about income and expenses. To allocate more of my time and energy to things that make me happy.

What are the areas in which you feel like a slave? What's tying you down? Blocking you? Where will you start seeking your freedom?

Hint No. 3: I want to Be Happy

Well, that's easy. If I want to be happy, I should do the things that make me happy.

What makes me happy? What are my favorite things?

Surprisingly, this question was harder than I thought it would be. The answers I thought would come pouring out of me like in Julie Andrews' "my favorite things" failed to materialize.

As usual, it was the trusty list that helped. It's always good to make a list, and the best lists take time, thought, and reflection.

What makes me happy? Here is my initial list:

- Playing games. Not every game, but there are some games I always love to play.

- Spending time with my family. It doesn't have to be a special vacation, even time at home is fun.

- Being alone for a couple of hours, at the beach if possible, with a cup of coffee if possible.

- Good music. Listening to good music and playing music too. Playing music with other people, playing in an ensemble.

- Good conversation with good friends, meeting good friends.

- Fruit salad can always make me happy, especially with yogurt and granola.

- An interesting project at work. A project in which I can express myself and that has a positive impact on the world. A project I do with people I enjoy working with and that is well paid.

That took me about 15 minutes, and I know it's only a partial list. Still, this list has already made a difference. There are several things I now know I want and am able to achieve, and that, in and of itself, is gladdening. **I try to focus on the things I can do, as opposed to the things that will make me happy if they happen, and which I have no control over.** This way my happiness is in my own hands, and not dependent on others. (There's an equally important list of happy things that happen without my intervention. That's the list of things I'm grateful for).

I leave my list open and get back to it over the next few days so that I'm able to expand on it, see if anything surprising comes to mind, and mostly use it as a reference. Best of all — I hang it on the refrigerator. It's at least as important as the shopping list.

Given time, the things you realize you love to do will multiply. Some things may even surprise you. Way back when I was 35, I made a list that contained a surprising item: "Learn how to play the drums". I had never played the drums before, but the desire has existed in the back of my mind ever since I was a child. There it lay dormant, until it was finally able to emerge and become apparent. I was, by then, a big enough child to decide to try. I took drumming lessons, and it turned out I was good enough to get together a group of talented friends and play covers to songs we loved. Those were very joyful moments.

Hint No. 4: I want to Do Good

Every time I do something, I want to do good:

Omelet? — Good omelet. Project at work? — Good project. I want to be a good dad, a good partner to my spouse, a good son, good in my profession, a good man.

I want to be good to myself and to others and do good for humanity. If I only knew what "Good" meant, I would certainly have a hint to the question "What do I want?"

How do I know what "Good" is?

The omelet is intuitive. I know what a good omelet is. But if my daughter asks me to drive her to school in the morning, so that she won't be late, things get complicated: Does being a good dad mean driving her to school (even though I don't want to), or letting her take the bus, thus taking responsibility for her tardiness? And yesterday: Was going to the beach for a couple of hours a good thing, even though I left a sink full of dishes I promised to wash? And right now: Is it good for me to eat the cake on the counter or to refrain from eating cake?

The answer (beware: cliche alert) comes from the heart. Our heart is the organ most adept at knowing good from bad. It will always surpass the mind and will leave our gut in the dust. In order to know what's good we should neither think nor follow our gut instincts. We need to (warning: prepare those sick bags) "listen to our hearts."

But this directive, besides making me nauseous, leaves me feeling helpless. I don't know how to listen to my heart. Fortunately, a friend gave me a different directive, one that works better for me. It's called "Ask Love". Do you want to know what is good? Ask what Love would do. In other words, what would you do if you were acting from a loving position, or if Love itself were acting for you?

So now I ask, and Love answers. This morning Love told me not to drive my daughter to school. It's better for both of us. Yesterday Love told me to go to the beach after I do the dishes, provided I still want to go to the beach. And right now Love is telling me I don't really want that piece of cake.

Ask Love, all its advice is given for free. It's free Love.

Hint No. 5: I Want Free Will

This whole book, front to back, hints at it all along: I want free will. I want to discover my free will at every given moment. I want to develop and grow through my new desires, I want to get to know myself better, and discover the purpose of my existence by having a deeper and finer understanding of my wishes and goals. I want to want. I want free will.

Will. Not urges or impulses. An urge, even though it comes from within, feels like an external force. I can respond to it or surrender to it. I never help it materialize. An urge arises from the place instincts come from — an almost animal place. There is no free will in an urge. I'm being pushed. Pushed to make a living, pushed to get things done, to satisfy or appease my environment. I don't take initiative. I'm pushed by instinct, social convention, or a fear greater than myself.

Will, not cravings. Cravings too, feel like an external power. If urges push, cravings pull. Like gravity. I follow them blindly; I'm drawn like a moth to a flame. Cravings dazzle and blind me. Cravings are childish, come from a small place within me, drawing me to the same things repeatedly. I'm drawn to screens, to thrills, to positive feedback, to chocolate. I know one square of chocolate is enough and that the second or third or eighth square will never be enough. I'll only suffer more. I may have eaten the first square out of free will, but from the second square on — it's my cravings that are managing me.

I want free will. Free will through which I am able to realize myself. Free will as the source of my happiness, the place I feel alive in and where I'm free. **Free will that is at a point of balance, where I'm neither pushed nor pulled, yet I'm also not standing still. I'm moving by the power of my own free will.**

Words for the Wise:

Yes, I (also) want to be content. I want to fulfill my wishes and feel satisfied. And if I'm not able to fulfill my current wishes, I want to be satisfied with those I have realized in the past. No matter what, I want to be content with fulfilling my wishes: How can I do that without knowing what I'm wishing for?

EPILOGUE:
7 MINUTES IN HEAVEN

Let's pretend you died and are standing at heaven's pearly gates. You're asked if there's anything else you still want to accomplish in life. What do you say?

Ingredients:

Wood to knock on

Directions:

1 Imagine you're standing on clouds, at heaven's gates, and an angel asks you if there's **anything you still really want to do, or experience, and that is worthy to return to life for and get done.** Something you still need to accomplish. An opportunity you might never forgive yourself for missing.

2 Take 7 minutes to answer the question.

3 Write down any answer that comes up: Big wishes, small desires, plans, dreams, ambitions — anything worth coming back to life for.

4 No answers? Don't worry. It doesn't mean you have nothing to live for, it only means this exercise isn't right for you at present. Try it again in 7 minutes, or in 7 hours, or in 7 years.

Tip:

Return to this exercise occasionally, because "Death…," as Elisabeth Kubler-Ross once said, "…is of vital importance."

Acknowledgements

Thank you to Noam Cohen, Tarika Zohar, Amos Avisar and my dear parents, for reading my early drafts and giving me valuable feedback.

Thank you to James Baraz and Uri Cohen, who shared their thoughts on free will and desire, as seen from their own personal worldviews (Buddhism and Anthroposophy, respectively).

A special thanks goes to Rabbi Elisha Wolfin, who very generously served as my editor. He read every word and suggested myriads of corrections, accuracies and improvements, while happily sharing his Pluralistic Jewish point of view.

My biggest thanks go to my three life partners, Michal, Inbal and Zohar. They both allowed and accommodated my year of self-discovery, and all the "hormonal changes" that were an inevitable part of this fascinating journey.

Made in the USA
Monee, IL
09 April 2025